ABOUT THIS BOOK

The illustrations for this book were done in Acryla Gouache on cold press illustration board, and then scanned and assembled in a digital collage. This book was edited by Nikki Garcia and designed by Véronique Lefèvre Sweet. The production was supervised by Patricia Alvarado, and the production editor was Jen Graham. The text was set in Goudy Old Style Bold, and the display type is Naive Inline Shadow Bold.

Little, Brown and Company • Hachette Book Group • 1290 Avenue of the Americas, New York, NY 10104 • Visit us at LBYR.com

First Edition: December 2021

Little, Brown and Company is a division of Hachette Book Group, Inc.
The Little, Brown name and logo are trademarks of Hachette Book Group, Inc.

The publisher is not responsible for websites (or their content) that are not owned by the publisher.

Library of Congress Cataloging-in-Publication Data
Names: Parsons, Karyn, 1968– author. | Christie, R. Gregory, 1971– illustrator.
Title: Saving the day : Garrett Morgan's life-changing invention of the traffic signal / by Karyn Parsons ; illustrated by R. Gregory Christie.
Description: First edition. | New York ; Boston : Little, Brown and Company, 2021. | Summary: "The story of Garrett Morgan, an African American inventor, who created the first automatic three-way traffic signal system." —Provided by publisher.
Identifiers: LCCN 2020032649 | ISBN 9780316457262 (hardcover) | Subjects: LCSH: Morgan, Garrett A., 1877–1963—Poetry—Juvenile literature. | African American inventors—Biography—Juvenile literature. | Inventors—United States—Biography—Juvenile literature. | Traffic signs and signals—Juvenile literature. | Historical poetry.
Classification: LCC TJ140.M67 P37 2021 | DDC 609.2 [B]—dc23
LC record available at https://lccn.loc.gov/2020032649

ISBN 978-0-316-45726-2

PRINTED IN CHINA

1010

10 9 8 7 6 5 4

SAVING THE DAY

GARRETT MORGAN'S LIFE-CHANGING INVENTION OF THE TRAFFIC SIGNAL

By **KARYN PARSONS**

Illustrated by **R. GREGORY CHRISTIE**

Little, Brown and Company

New York Boston

Morning dawned,
And the sun's golden rays
Signaled to Garrett Morgan
That it was a new day.

With his head in the clouds,
Always full of a dream,
He was no help to others,
Or so it seemed.

His brothers and sisters
Worked the house and the field.
But Garrett's talents
Had yet to be revealed.

He fell off all ladders.
Couldn't hammer a nail.
Was too weak to lift things,
Not even a pail.

They'd all say, "Run along.
Go be by yourself."
And though he liked dreaming,
He wanted to help.

He'd spend time alone.
Long walks he would take,
His mind imagining
New creations to make.

In the middle of the road
A wheel lay on the ground.
"I know I can use that."
So Garrett bent down.

But sometimes his dreaming
Got him into trouble.
He wouldn't watch where he was going,
His mind in a bubble.

See, along came a car,
From the side a red truck.
And though they missed Garrett,
Their nerves had been struck.

Both slammed on their brakes,
Dodged the boy by a hair.
But the near collision
Gave everyone a scare.

Back at home, his mom said,
"You wait here for your dad."
He just knew he was in trouble,
That his parents were mad.

His father walked in,
Looked at Garrett a beat,
Then called him over.
"Come here, son. Have a seat.

"You have a great mind.
Imaginative, keen.
Ready to invent new
From what has not yet been seen.

"Yes, you have a great mind
But could do even more.
A tutor in the city
Could help your dreams soar.

"This decision was hard.
We don't want you away.
But it's for your own good.
You'll understand one day."

Then Garrett's mother
Pulled him close, and she said,
"But always remember this, son.
Keep this in your head.

"While Ruth's good at fishing,
And Will likes to bake,
Lucille loves the stars
and the patterns they make.

"Frank's good with tools,
Can fix anything.
And Minnie's at her best
When she can sing.

"You, too, son, have something
That's all yours alone.
Something to contribute
That's just not yet known.

"All are given a gift.
Something you cannot learn.
It's what you do with that gift
That's your gift in return."

The city was loud,
People everywhere.
And cars and horses
And bicycles were there.

All on the same roads,
All at the same time.
Horns honking, cars crashing,
No reason or rhyme.

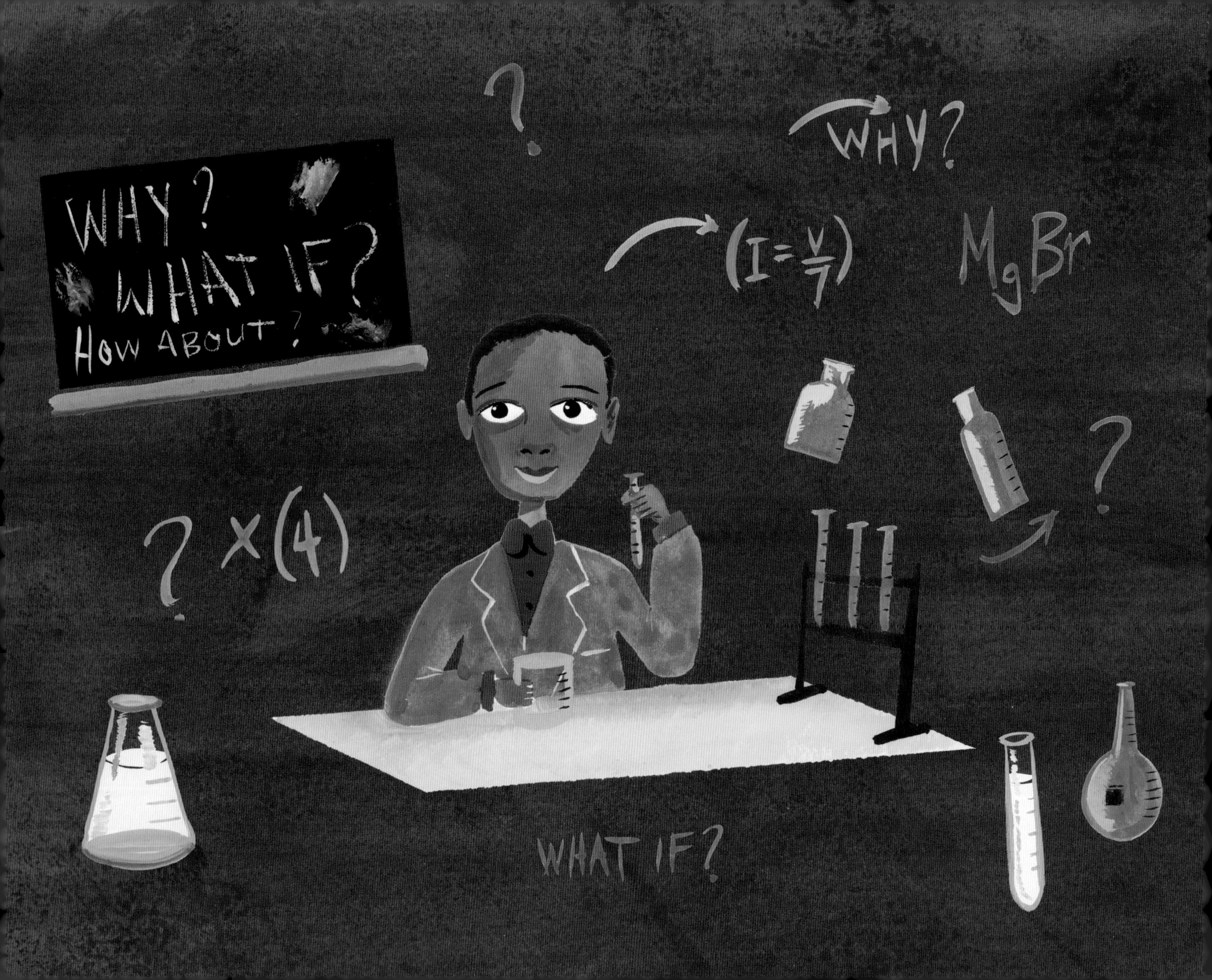

WHY?
WHAT IF?
HOW ABOUT?
WHY?
$(I = \frac{V}{7})$
MgBr
? x(4)
WHAT IF?

Garrett studied hard,
And when his lessons were done,
He found a job
Doing something he found fun.

Fixing sewing machines,
With their rotors and springs
And gears and buttons,
Made him think of many things.

Like a new kind of stitch
On the sewing machine,
One that made zigzags
And kept edges clean.

His mind churned and churned
With new ideas to invent.
Some drew attention.
Some helped pay the rent.

But Garrett didn't care about fame
Or about wealth.
What he wanted most
Was to show he could help.

The day's early dawn
Signaled Garrett to wake.
He decided to walk.
A scenic route he would take.

The grass, sparkling green,
Had just been cut low.
Garrett longed to run through it.
He decided to go.

But just as he started,
A white car whizzed past,
Heading for the crosswalk
And going quite fast.

Then he heard tires screech
And someone yell, "STOP!"
A horse and carriage were approaching.
He could hear the hooves clop.

But the horse kept on going,
Didn't even slow down.
Garrett ran fast to warn them
But soon heard the sound.

First a *CRASH!* and a *BOOM!*
Then the horse whinnied high.
When Garrett finally got there,
He tried not to cry.

Though everyone was okay,
And the horse would be all right,
He'd seen too many wrecks.
It was a terrible sight.

That day as he worked
On a sewing machine,
His mind drifted back to
The collision he'd seen.

"There has to be some way
To let drivers know
That someone else is approaching.
When to stop and to go.

"And a signal before stopping
So first they could slow down.
But they'd have to see it;
It couldn't only be sound."

But as Garrett wandered home,
Ideas in his head flowing,
He forgot to pay attention
To just where he was going.

He stepped off a curb.
The bike signaled, no doubt.
He saw a bright light,
And then he went out.

His mind was filled
With colorful light.
On and then off.
What a beautiful sight.

The green grass of a field,
Illuminated by sun,
Shone bright
And invited Garrett to run.

Golden light through the window
Eased in the morning.
A new day was beginning.
It was a subtle warning.

The red glow of the coals
Far too hot to touch
Told Garrett to stop.
One more move was too much.

His mind was racing,
Ideas twisted and knotted.
Then he suddenly jumped up and exclaimed,
"I've got it!!!

"A TRAFFIC SIGNAL!"
That's what he'd create
So all could travel safely.
Yes! It'd be great!

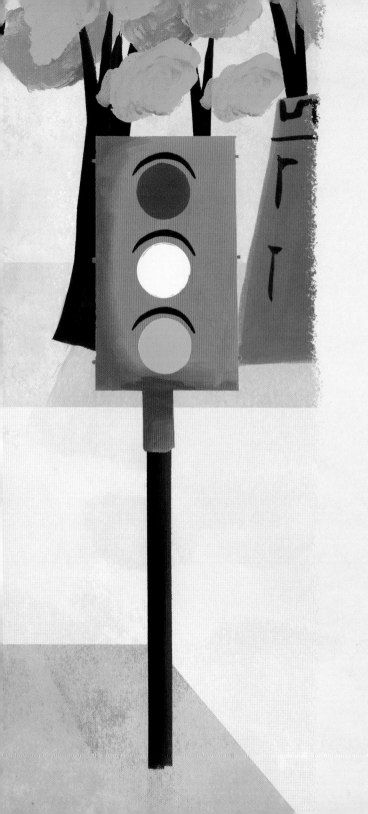

The red, yellow, and green
Would come along later,
But it was Garrett's foundation
That made us all safer.

Garrett had a gift.
Yes, that is a fact.
But what meant the most
Was that he gave back.

AUTHOR'S NOTE

IN THE YEARS THAT I'VE WORKED TO BRING THE STORIES OF LITTLE-KNOWN AFRICAN AMERICAN INNOVATORS AND HEROES TO CHILDREN AND THEIR FAMILIES, I've discovered countless Black inventors whose contributions are often everyday items that we take for granted. Some are simple objects used around the house, while others are far more complex.

When I would share the accomplishments and innovations of Black people that I'd unearthed, I sometimes found my enthusiasm met with silence. A cloud of doubt. Many found it impossible to believe that Black people were capable of doing great things. The shocked responses that I receive from children, and adults, when they hear about Garrett Morgan make me see how necessary it is for these stories to be shared with young readers.

Morgan came from a big family. He was a gifted inventor—an observer who focused on fixing problems. He was inspired to create a T-shaped traffic signal that had a "caution" warning after witnessing an accident at a problematic intersection. In between these truths, I imagined this story to highlight how Morgan was able to do something great and important by focusing his creative energy. Because this is a book for children, I wrote Morgan's story in rhyme, and the dialogue is not verbatim. Instead, the dialogue represents the spirit of what was said throughout Morgan's life.

When I decided to share Morgan's story as a Sweet Blackberry short film, I had a hard time sticking simply to his invention of the traffic signal, because his contributions to our everyday life are vast and varied. Ultimately, focusing on Morgan's traffic signal made the most sense. After all, Sweet Blackberry's audience is made up of young children who are fairly new to navigating busy streets and crosswalks.

But Morgan invented products, accomplished extraordinary things, and embarked on ventures throughout his impressive life. Most notable was his invention of a breathing device that he called the Morgan Safety Hood and Smoke Protector. It would later be dubbed the gas mask, the blueprint of which would be used to provide American soldiers with protection during World War I. Morgan was also a dedicated activist. He faced tremendous racism as he made strides in business, but through activism and politics he used the success he had achieved to help fight for equal rights and opportunities for African Americans.

In 1923, Morgan would patent the traffic signal. There had been versions of a machine to help mitigate traffic before his, but Morgan's invention offered a three-way traffic signal (what is now the yellow-light system) allowing drivers a warning, giving them time to stop. The red, yellow, and green traffic light we know today would come after Morgan's invention; however, his mechanism is the foundation for that stoplight.

Morgan took his talent, along with his successes and failures, and found a way to always give back. I invite you to learn more about his impressive life. A true gift indeed!

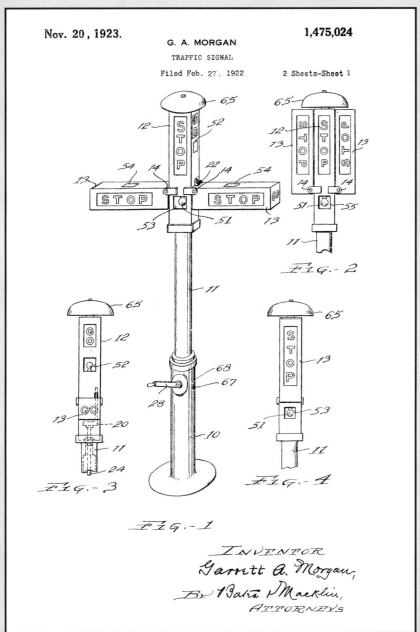

The official patent for Morgan's traffic signal invention. *(Courtesy of the United States Patent and Trademark Office)*

Morgan circa 1950 in a suit with a medal pinned to it. *(Photo by Fotosearch/Getty Images)*